MY CANADA

SASKATCHEWAN

Weigl

Published by Weigl Educational Publishers Limited
6325 10th Street SE
Calgary, Alberta T2H 2Z9

Website: www.weigl.ca

Library and Archives Canada Cataloguing in Publication

Goldsworthy, Kaite, author
     Saskatchewan / Kaite Goldsworthy.

(My Canada)
ISBN 978-1-77071-878-4 (bound).--ISBN 978-1-77071-879-1 (pbk.)

     1. Saskatchewan--Juvenile literature. I. Title. II. Series: My
Canada (Calgary, Alta.)

FC3511.2.G65 2013   j971.24   C2013-902399-2

Printed in the United States of America in North Mankato, Minnesota
1 2 3 4 5 6 7 8 9 0   17 16 15 14 13

052013
WEP040413

Project Coordinator: Megan Cuthbert
Art Director: Terry Paulhus

Weigl acknowledges Getty Images as the primary image
supplier for this title.

We acknowledge the financial support of the Government
of Canada through the Canada Book Fund for our
publishing activities.

2

Contents

3

This is Saskatchewan. It was named by the Cree people. The name means swiftly flowing river.

This is the shape of Saskatchewan. Saskatchewan is between Alberta and Manitoba. They are the three Prairie Provinces.

The Northwest Territories is north of Saskatchewan.

UNITED STATES

Northwest Territories

Alberta

Manitoba

Saskatchewan

CANADA

N

UNITED STATES

Regina is the capital city of Saskatchewan. It is sometimes called the Queen City.

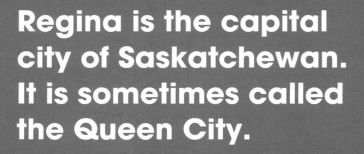

The city of Regina was first called Pile of Bones.

The Royal Canadian Mounted Police Training Academy is in Regina. All of Canada's RCMP have trained there since 1885.

Many people visit the RCMP Heritage Centre in Regina every year.

The province's coat of arms has a green shield with three gold wheat sheaves. A lion and a deer are on each side of the shield. At the top is a beaver wearing a crown.

The beaver is a symbol of Canada. Beavers live in every province and territory of Canada.

This is the flag of Saskatchewan. It is green and gold with a red flower on the right side. The shield of arms is in the top left corner.

The green on the flag is for the forests of Saskatchewan.

The white-tailed deer is Saskatchewan's official animal. It lifts its tail up when it is scared. The deer can be found all over the province.

The flower of Saskatchewan is the western red lily. It grows in the meadows and woods of the province.

18 content

Half of Canada's wheat is grown in Saskatchewan. Wheat is used to make bread, pasta, and other food.

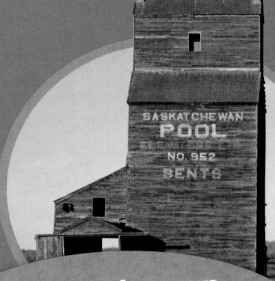

Saskatchewan has many large grain elevators. Grain elevators were once used to store wheat.

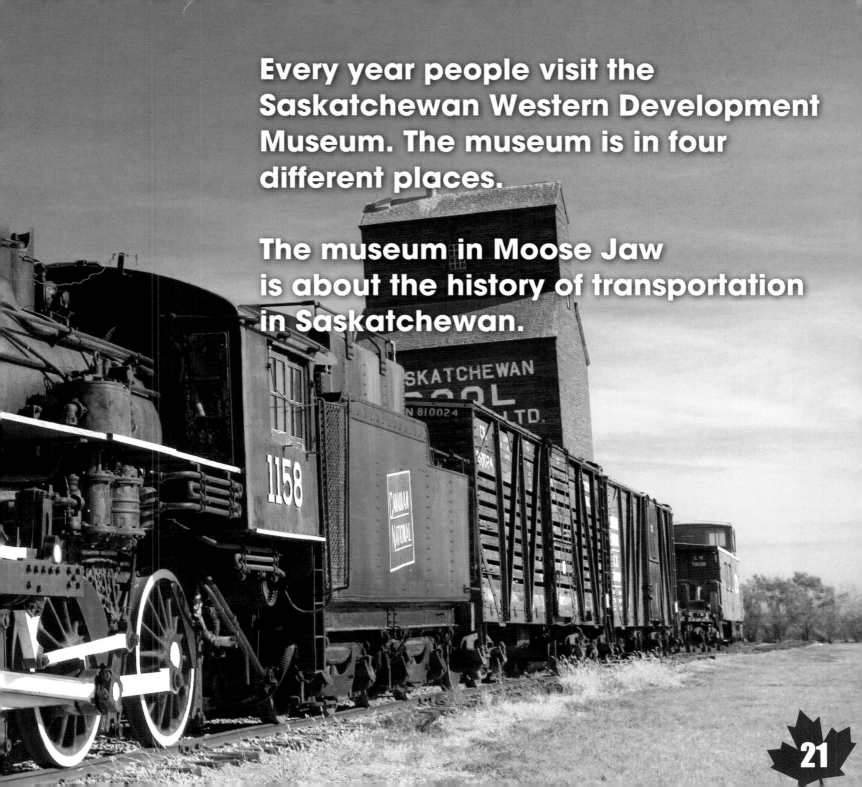

Every year people visit the Saskatchewan Western Development Museum. The museum is in four different places.

The museum in Moose Jaw is about the history of transportation in Saskatchewan.

SASKATCHEWAN FACTS

These pages provide detailed information that expands on the interesting facts found in the book. They are intended to be used by adults as a learning support to help young readers round out their knowledge of each province and territory in the *My Canada* series.

Pages 4–5

"Swiftly flowing river" refers to the Saskatchewan River, which flows through the province. Saskatchewan is 651,036 square kilometres in area. It has a population of more than 1 million people. The province has more than 100,000 lakes and rivers. It also has 250,000 kilometres of road surface, more than any other province.

Pages 6–7

Saskatchewan is the middle Prairie Province. It is one of only two land-locked provinces. Lake Athabasca extends across the border between Saskatchewan and Alberta. It is 7,935 square kilometres and is the eighth largest lake in Canada. The sand dunes that stretch for 100 kilometres beside the lake are the only active dunes in Canada.

Pages 8–9

Regina is Latin for "queen," and the city was named in honour of Queen Victoria. Regina was originally known as "Pile of Bones" due to the large buffalo bone piles left there by First Nations hunters. Regina became the provincial capital in 1906. It has a population of more than 200,000. The city has more than 350,000 trees and 600 parks.

Pages 10–11

The RCMP training centre, or "Depot" division, in Regina provides basic training for all RCMP cadets. It was originally the headquarters for the North West Mounted Police, later the Royal Northwest Mounted Police. The 21,000-square-metre RCMP Heritage Centre has displays and exhibits documenting the history of the RCMP. The centre was opened in Regina in 2007 and is located on the grounds of the RCMP Academy.

Pages 12–13

The sheaves of wheat on Saskatchewan's shield represent agriculture. The royal lion and white-tailed deer wear Prairie Aboriginal beadwork collars in reference to the province's Métis and First Nations peoples. The provincial motto, "From Many Peoples Strength," refers to the province's multicultural heritage.

Pages 14–15

The green on the flag represents the forests in northern Saskatchewan, while the gold represents the wheat grown in the south. The flower is the western red lily. A contest was held to design the provincial flag. The winning flag design was chosen out of more than 4,000 entries. It was adopted in 1969.

Pages 16–17

The white-tailed deer gets its name from the white underside of its tail and rump. The deer can weigh up to 180 kilograms. It is a popular game animal in the province. It is also the most widely found large animal in North America. The western red lily grows in moist areas. Flowers bloom in June and July, producing six reddish-orange petals.

Pages 18–19

Saskatchewan produces more than half of the wheat grown in Canada and 10 percent of the world's exported wheat. There were once more than 3,000 grain elevators in the province, but only about 400 remain. As bigger companies have taken over smaller operations, many grain elevators are no longer needed.

Pages 20–21

The Saskatchewan Western Development Museum was founded in 1949. Each of the locations tells a different part of Saskatchewan's history. North Battleford is a heritage farm and village, Saskatoon has a recreated 1910 'boomtown,' and Yorkton tells about the immigrant experience. Every year, 200,000 people visit the museum locations.

KEY WORDS

Research has shown that as much as 65 percent of all written material published in English is made up of 300 words. These 300 words cannot be taught using pictures or learned by sounding them out. They must be recognized by sight. This book contains 59 common sight words to help young readers improve their reading fluency and comprehension. This book also teaches young readers several important content words, such as proper nouns. These words are paired with pictures to aid in learning and improve understanding.

Page	Sight Words First Appearance
4	by, is, it, means, named, people, river, the, this, was
7	and, are, between, of, they, three
8	city, first, sometimes
11	all, every, have, in, many, there, year
12	a, at, each, has, on, side, with
13	live
15	for, left, right
16	all, animal, be, can, found, its, over, up, when
17	grows
19	food, large, make, once, other, to, used, were
21	about, different, four, places

Page	Content Words First Appearance
4	Cree, Saskatchewan
7	Alberta, Manitoba, Northwest Territories, Prairie Provinces, shape, United States
8	Pile of Bones, Regina
11	Canada, RCMP Heritage Centre, Royal Canadian Mounted Police Training Academy
12	beaver, coat of arms, crown, deer, lion, shield, top, wheat sheaves
13	symbol, territory
15	corner, flag, flower, forests
16	tail
17	meadows, western red lily, woods
19	bread, elevators, pasta, wheat
21	history, Moose Jaw, Saskatchewan Western Development Museum, transportation

WEBSITES

To learn more about Saskatchewan, visit these websites.

Encyclopedia of Saskatchewan
http://esask.uregina.ca/home.html

Government of Saskatchewan
http://www.gov.sk.ca/fun-zone/

Tourism Saskatchewan
http://www.sasktourism.com/about-saskatchewan/quick-facts